THEMATIC UNIT
My Country

Written Cynthia Holzschuher

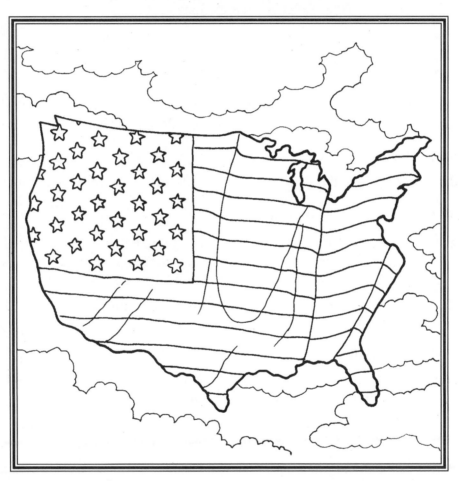

Teacher Created Resources, Inc.
6421 Industry Way
Westminster, CA 92683
www.teachercreated.com

©1996 Teacher Created Resources, Inc.
Reprinted, 2005

Made in U.S.A.
ISBN-1-55734-586-4

Illustrated by
Karon Walstad

Edited by
Barbara M. Wally

Cover Art by
Agi Palinay

Table of Contents

Introduction

My Country is a captivating, whole-language, thematic unit celebrating the United States: her leaders, music, holidays, and monuments. It contains 80 pages of lesson designs and reproducible activities for use in the primary classroom. At its core are three high-quality children's literature selections: *Oh, What a Thanksgiving!, George Washington: A Picture Book Biography,* and *The Star-Spangled Banner.* Ideas and activities which set the stage for reading, encourage enjoyment of the book, and extend the concepts are included for each book. The unit also connects the theme to areas of the curriculum with activities in language arts, math, social studies, science, art, music, and life skills. Many of these activities encourage cooperative learning. Suggestions and patterns for a bulletin board, game board, and book report form are unit management tools which will help the busy teacher. The culminating activity will allow the students to synthesize their knowledge in a creative experience highlighting the important aspects of a colonial child's day.

The lessons are arranged chronologically, from the first colonists through the early 1800s. However, each section is complete and may be used alone or in any order appropriate for your classroom needs.

This thematic unit includes:

❏ **literature selections**—summaries of three children's books with related lessons and activities that cross the curriculum

❏ **writing and language experience ideas**—daily suggestions, as well as writing activities across the curriculum

❏ **poetry**—lessons for theme related poetry selections

❏ **planning guides**—suggestions for sequencing lessons each day of the unit

❏ **curriculum connections**—in language arts, math, social studies, science, art, music, and life skills

❏ **bulletin board**—suggestions for a student-created bulletin board

❏ **a culminating activity**—which requires students to synthesize their learning to engage in an activity that can be shared with others

❏ **a bibliography**—suggesting additional literature related to the theme

---

To keep this valuable resource intact so that it can be used year after year, you may wish to punch holes in the pages and store them in a three-ring binder.

Introduction *(cont.)*

Why Whole Language?

Selected literature is central to the whole-language approach. Through literature children become involved in all modalities of communication: reading, writing, listening, observing, doing, experiencing, and illustrating. Reading and language skills, formerly taught in isolation, are combined as the child responds to literature by reading, writing (spelling appropriately for his/her level), speaking, listening, etc. In this way, language skills develop naturally, stimulated by personal interest and involvement in a specific topic.

Why Thematic Planning?

Thematic planning is a very useful tool for implementing an integrated whole-language program. By choosing a theme with correlating literature selections for a unit of study, a teacher can plan activities throughout the day that lead to a cohesive, in-depth study of the topic. Students tend to learn and retain more when they are applying their skills in an interesting and meaningful context. Both teachers and students will be freed from a day that is broken into unrelated segments of isolated drill and practice.

Why Cooperative Learning?

Students need to learn social skills as well as academic skills and content. No longer can this area of development be taken for granted. Students must learn to work cooperatively in groups in order to function well in modern society. Group activities should be a regular part of school life, and teachers should consciously include social objectives as well as academic objectives in their planning. For example, a group working together to solve a problem may need to select a leader. The teacher should make clear to the students the qualities of good leader-follower group interaction and monitor them just as he/she would state and monitor the academic goals of the project.

Why Big Books?

An excellent cooperative, whole-language activity is the production of Big Books. Groups of students, or the whole class, can apply their language skills, content knowledge, and creativity to produce a Big Book that can become a part of the classroom library to be read and reread. These books make excellent culminating projects for sharing beyond the classroom with parents, librarians, other classes, etc. Big Books can be produced in many ways, and this thematic unit book includes directions for at least one method you may choose.

Why Journals?

Each day your students should have the opportunity to write in a journal. They may respond to a book or a historical event, write about a personal experience, or answer a general "question of the day" posed by the teacher. The cumulative journal provides an excellent means of documenting writing progress.

1776–USA is Born

Introduction *(cont.)*

Learning Centers

A learning center is a special area of the classroom set aside for the study of a specific topic. It contains a variety of materials that teach, reinforce, and enrich skills and provides an easy means of accommodating students with different abilities and learning styles. Activities in each center should be selected and prepared based on the interests and needs of the students in your class. Centers are appropriate for both individuals and cooperative groups.

Here are some suggestions for learning center activities appropriate for this unit.

Literature and Life Skills Reading

Provide a collection of fiction and nonfiction books about the United States (see bibliography). You may want to tape record some of the most popular ones for use in a listening center. In addition, it is important to have multiple copies of some selections for group reading. Have reading records, book report forms, and bookmarks (pages 69–71) available in the center so that students may record their own progress. During the Thanksgiving section of the unit, you may wish to provide grocery advertisements for practice "shopping" or writing grocery lists. Simple cookbooks and magazines can be included for reading recipes, abbreviations, directions, etc.

Writing

Students should write or dictate stories every day. Make map shape books, using the pattern on page 38 for the cover and to cut lined paper, or make simple blank books from handwriting paper with red and blue construction paper covers. Post the word bank from page 9 for spelling help.

Art/Music

Prepare one or more of the suggested art activities for use by students in this center. In addition, you may provide a recorder and tapes for listening to a variety of patriotic music (*Wee Sing America* by Pamela Conn Beall and Susan Hagen Nipp, Price Stern Sloan, 1-800-421-0892). For a manipulative activity, prepare the word strips for "The Star-Spangled Banner," page 33.

Life Skills

If it is practical, the children will enjoy a free time center with several colonial and Native American games. You may use the suggestions on page 65 or research others (see bibliography).

Social Studies Games

Prepare the Monument Picture Match game cards on page 53 and the patriotic board game on pages 73–75. These can be used by small groups of students to reinforce learning.

Oh, What a Thanksgiving!

by Steven Kroll

Summary

This is the story of a boy with a remarkable imagination. He becomes interested in Thanksgiving during a history lesson and projects himself back to the time of the Pilgrims. David pretends to be involved in the planning and preparation of the first Thanksgiving and finds it to be even more fun than his family's modern activities. The reader has an opportunity to compare past and present traditions and learn about historical figures associated with the holiday.

The plan below suggests a schedule for using the activities in this unit. You may adapt them to your situation as you choose.

Sample Plan

Day 1

- Put up the Thanksgiving bulletin board (pages 76–77).
- Discuss Thanksgiving traditions (page 7).
- Trace the Pilgrim's route to America.
- Read *Oh, What a Thanksgiving!* to the class.
- Complete the Story Frames activity on page page 16.
- Begin a three-section chart (page 7) and ask for student responses and questions.

Day 2

- Assign one of the Daily Writing Activities (page 37).
- Reread the pages of the book that are about colonial times.
- Reread the parts about a modern Thanksgiving.
- Complete the Then and Now activity page (page 13).
- Make a cornhusk doll or a humming toy (page 61).
- Plant corn, following the directions on page 50.

Day 3

- Continue Daily Writing Activities (page 37).
- Make the Story Props on pages 10–11. Retell the story. Work in groups to make pop-up books (page 12) of original Thanksgiving stories (colonial or modern).
- Brainstorm a list of common or favorite dinner foods.
- Complete the Shop for Dinner activity (page 14).
- Do the Taste Without Smell experiment (page 52).
- Brainstorm items for a Venn diagram (page 15), comparing and contrasting Thanksgiving then and now.

Day 4

- Continue Daily Writing Activities (page 37).
- Read "Over the River and Through the Wood" (page 34). Complete the activity and learn the song.
- Begin working on a colonial sampler (page 62).
- Make the Pilgrim hats and collars (pages 59–60).
- Make a compass (page 49).
- Complete the Pilgrim chart to be sure all the questions have been answered.

Overview of Activities

SETTING THE STAGE

1. Make the bulletin board, pages 76–77, and learning centers, page 5. Contact your librarian for a collection of appropriate reading materials. Send home the letter to parents, page 68, announcing the unit and requesting help with the culminating activity.

2. Locate England, Holland, and Plymouth, Massachusetts, on a map of the world. Trace the Pilgrims' journey. Discuss how they traveled and how we would travel the same route today.

3. Make the pocket chart on page 9. Brainstorm a list of Thanksgiving theme words to post as a word bank for writing assignments. Have children classify the words as foods and non-foods or nouns/verbs. Have each student make a small pictionary of Thanksgiving words, using the word bank.

4. Encourage your students to share family Thanksgiving traditions. How are they the same? different? Make pictures of families enjoying Thanksgiving dinner.

ENJOYING THE BOOK

1. Read the story, *Oh, What a Thanksgiving!*, paying careful attention to the illustrations. Discuss life then and now. Have the children complete the story frame, page 16, or make an entry in their journals telling about their imaginary Pilgrim life.

2. Make an inquiry chart on poster board or on the chalkboard. Title the chart PILGRIMS and make three columns. Label the columns: What I Know, What I'd Like to Know, What I Learned. Record information in phrases and continue to fill in the chart throughout the study of the book and holiday. Use a different color of marker or chalk each day so that students can see the information build.

3. Reread the book pages that are about colonial times. Then read the pages about modern Thanksgiving. Make pop-up books (see page 12) and have students write original Thanksgiving stories.

4. Make a list of the "doing" words (verbs) associated with Thanksgiving that are found in the book: i.e., shopping, teaching, cooking, eating, etc. Use each word in a sentence.

5. Follow the directions on page 50 to plant corn as the Pilgrims did. Display and discuss other foods that are native to America, like turkey, pumpkin, cranberries, tomatoes, and potatoes.

6. The Indians brought popped corn to the first Thanksgiving. It became a favorite with the colonists and was eaten like cereal for breakfast or for dinner. Share a treat of popcorn to celebrate like the Pilgrims did! As an extension, make extra popcorn and decorate pictures with the popcorn. Write stories about the pictures.

7. The Pilgrims used a compass to find their way across the ocean. Use the activity on page 49 to make a compass. Discuss direction and magnetism.

Overview of Activities *(cont.)*

EXTENDING THE BOOK

1. Have students make cornhusk dolls or humming toys, page 61. Read about the games of colonial children, page 65, and set up an area in the classroom for free time play.

2. Use the Story Props on pages 10–11 to make posters and dioramas or have the children work in groups to plan puppet shows or art projects. You may wish to assign the writing of simple dialog for retelling the story. Children may present the puppet show or display their art work at the culminating activity.

3. Complete the Shop for Dinner activity, page 14. Brainstorm a list of favorite foods. Classify them as breakfast, lunch, or dinner. Extend the activity by collecting empty grocery packages, pricing them, and role playing supermarket "shopping." More advanced students may enjoy using coupons and calculators.

4. Indians introduced corn or maise to the Pilgrims, and it quickly became a favorite food. Brainstorm a list of the ways that we eat corn today: on the cob, popped, corn flakes, corn muffins, etc. Take a survey of favorite corn foods and make a graph of the results.

5. Read about some other early colonies. Jamestown was founded in 1607. Make a Venn diagram to compare life in two or more colonies. The Pilgrims in Massachusetts were stern and strict. Was that true of settlers in Jamestown, Virginia?

6. Write an American cinquain, pages 35–36, using Pilgrims or things associated with Thanksgiving as the subject. Frame the poems in the turkey pattern (page 70) and make a display in the classroom or make them into a Big Book.

7. Make the Pilgrim hats and collars, pages 59–60, to use at the culminating activities.

8. Girls in colonial America learned by making samplers. Have students follow the directions on page 62 to create a sampler.

9. Pilgrims found a small, sour, red berry, which they called "craneberry" because it resembled the long neck and head of a crane. Native Americans used the cranberry juice to dye rugs and blankets and also to heal wounds. Ripened wild cranberries were eaten fresh or ground or mashed with corn meal and baked into bread. Word of this delicious fruit reached Europe, and cranberries were in demand there. Today cranberries are often eaten at Thanksgiving. Choose a favorite cranberry recipe and prepare it in class.

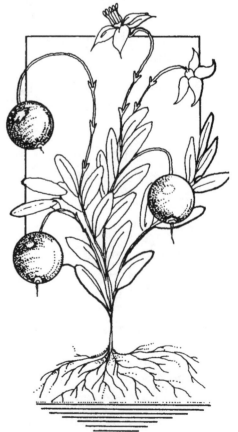

Making a Pocket Chart

It is quick and easy to make a pocket chart if you have access to a laminator. Begin by laminating a 24" x 36" (61 cm x 91 cm) piece of colored tagboard. Run about 18 inches (46 cm) of additional plastic. Cut the clear plastic into nine equal strips. Space the strips equally along the long side of tagboard and attach them with cellophane tape along the bottom and sides. The pockets will hold sentence strips, vocabulary cards, or an eight-line poem plus title. The chart can be displayed in a learning center or used with a group.

Here are some ideas for using your pocket chart:

- print patriotic song words on sentence strips
- provide word cards (out of order) for students to sequence into sentences
- order the lines of a poem
- display appropriate theme vocabulary as a spelling aid for creative writing
- display a group of number facts which have 13 as the answer

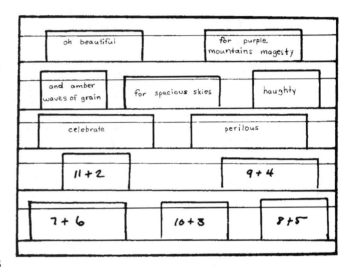

You may also use the pocket chart to display vocabulary words and definitions. Here are suggested word lists for each of the books in this unit:

Oh, What a Thanksgiving!

voyage	harbor	survivors	celebrate	cottage
thatched	aisles	bustled	venison	unfamiliar
clapboard	musket	commander	breeches	appreciating

George Washington

minister	survey	seizures	fleet	electors
marksman	tragedy	retreat	delegates	ballots
hounds	militia	allies	harpsichord	retire

The Star-Spangled Banner (vs. 1)

hailed	perilous	mists	reposes	conceal
twilight	gallantly	foe	towering	disclose
gleaming	dimly	haughty	fitfully	reflected

Story Props

Color, cut out, and glue these patterns to tagboard. Laminate them for durability. Add a craft stick to the bottom, if desired. Use these patterns in dioramas, pop-up books, posters, or as puppets.

Story Props *(cont.)*

Pop-up Books and Cards

Have students make pop-up books in which to write original stories. Each student can contribute a page to a class pop-up book. You may wish to have students work in small groups.
Pop-up books and cards can be used throughout the school year for a number of activities and purposes.

Materials: several pieces of 9" x 12" (23 cm x 30 cm) white construction paper (use other colors as needed), crayons, colored pencils or markers, glue, scissors

Directions:

1. Have students fold a piece of construction paper in half and cut slits down from the fold.

2. Help students push the cut area through the fold and crease it to form a pop-up section.

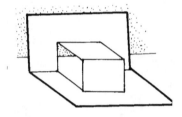

3. Have students make other pop-up pages and glue them back to back.

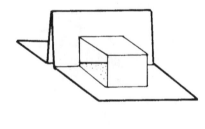

4. Help students glue a cover to their pop-up books.

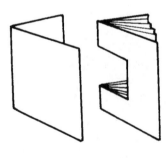

Help students write sentences above or below the pop-up section and glue an appropriate picture to the pop-up section of the page. (Make sure students' pictures are small enough to fit on the pop-up section.)

To create a pop-up card, follow steps one and two. Then, cut a cover the same size as the construction paper used in step 1, add a design or title, and glue it behind the pop-up section.

Then and Now

Draw pictures to show your answers.

Transportation

then | now

Cooking

then | now

Clothing

then | now

Home

then | now

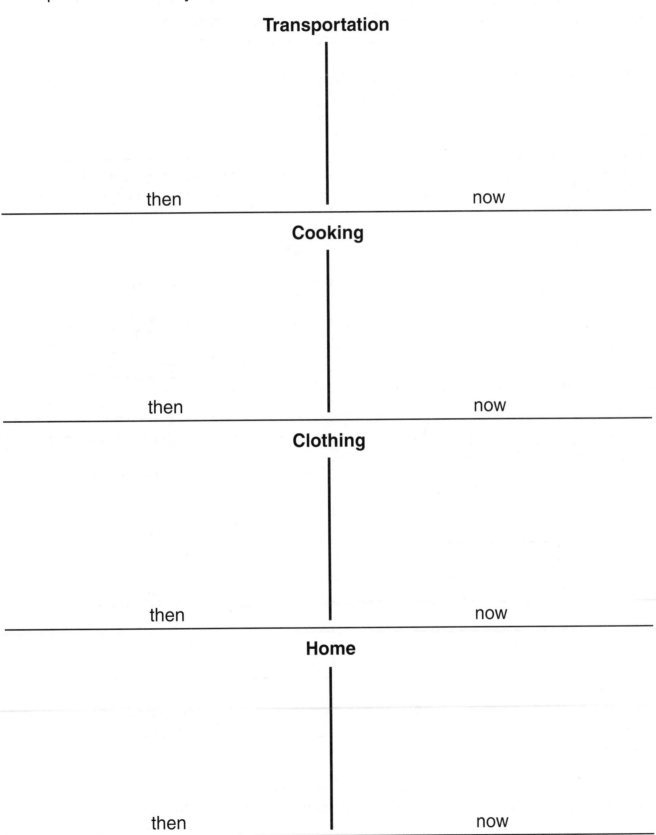

*(**Teacher**: Add appropriate prices before distributing this sheet.)*

Shop for Dinner

What foods would you buy for Thanksgiving dinner? Select foods to write on the shopping lists below. Add up the total cost.

Food	Cost
_____	_____
_____	_____
_____	_____
_____	_____
_____	_____
Total	_____

Venn Diagram

Complete the diagram to show what is the same and what is different between the first Thanksgiving and our modern Thanksgiving. Use the words below to fill in the diagram. Add any others you can think of.

turkey
corn
pumpkin
cranberries
Indian guests
family

friends
football games
parades
sweaters
tennis shoes
doublet

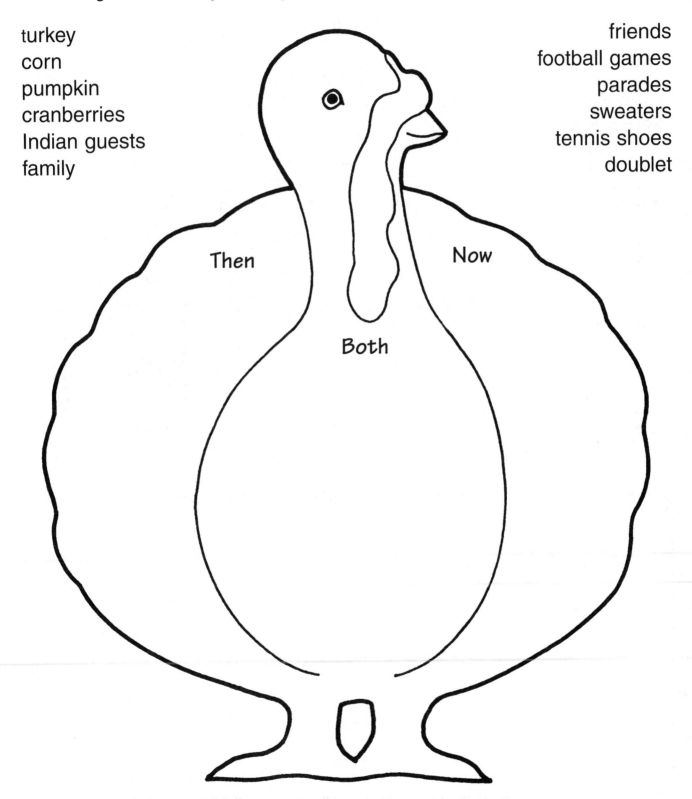

Then

Now

Both

Story Frames

Complete one of these story frames.

If I were a man in colonial America, I would like to live in _____ in the

year _____ . I would have a wife named _____ and

children named _____ and _____ .

In my fields I would plant _____ and _____ .

My most important tool would be a _____ . I would use it to

_____ . I would like to thank the Indians for _____ .

- *(cut apart)* -

If I were a woman in colonial America, I would like to live in _____

in the year _____ . I would have a husband named _____

and children named _____ and _____ .

Every day I would do chores like _____ and _____

to help my family. My most valuable possession would be a _____ .

It is important because _____ . I would like to thank the

Indians for _____ .

George Washington: A Picture Book Biography

by James Cross Giblin

Summary

George Washington was born on February 22, 1732, in the English colony of Virginia. At age 21 he joined the army and fought on the side of England in the French and Indian War. He was a good leader and a brave soldier. He married Martha Custis, a young widow with two children. The family moved to Mt. Vernon. When the war between England and the colonies began in 1775, George Washington became the leader of the Army. After eight years the colonies won the war, and George Washington was a hero. He was elected the first president of the United States in 1789 and lived in the country's capital, New York City. Later, a new capital city was built on the Potomac River and named in his honor.

The plan below suggests a schedule for using the activities in this unit. You may adapt them to your situation as you choose.

Sample Plan

Day 1
- Do Setting the Stage activities (page 18).
- Read *George Washington: A Picture Book Biography* to page 15.
- Write stories about Washington's family life.
- Begin a list of important events in George Washington's life.
- Discuss the job of a surveyor. Complete the survey activity (page 45).
- Make a hornbook (page 22) and use it to write vocabulary words.

Day 2
- Finish reading the story.
- Complete the story web, page 23.
- Complete the list of events in the life of George Washington.
- Do People and Places Word Search (page 41).
- Have children choose one event in Washington's life to illustrate and write about. Combine the pages in sequential order for a Big Book.
- Complete the Lucky 13 math activity, page 47, and design a 13-star flag.

Day 3
- Make a list of things the soldiers would have needed to survive at Valley Forge.

Compare and contrast their needs with your own in a Venn diagram (page 15).
- Write a story about the war from the viewpoint of a soldier. How did he feel about George Washington?
- Make Continental and British soldiers (page 24).

Day 4
- Complete the It's the Law! activity (page 25).
- Make antique paper and ink (page 43). Write with a quill pen.
- Enjoy a "tea party" (page 51) and research the Boston Tea Party. Write a class story about the experience.
- Share other books about the life and times of George Washington (see bibliography).
- Make a 13-star flag (page 57).
- Complete the map of the thirteen original colonies (page 55).

Day 5
- Make a model of the Washington Monument (page 39).
- Read about how a new city became the capital of the United States.
- Select a famous American for a report or project (page 54). Organize the written reports into a Big Book.
- Count coin combinations (page 46).

Overview of Activities

SETTING THE STAGE

1. Add the colonial soldier to the bulletin board. Show it to the class and explain that many people came to America after the Pilgrims did. By George Washington's time, there were several cities and towns. Enlarge the colonial map on page 55 to show where people lived.

2. Tell the children that for a long time people in America were governed by the King of England. Explain that after a war with England, the colonies formed a new country called the United States of America, with a new kind of government.

3. Show the book to the class and explain that this book is about the first president of the United States. Do they know what the president does or where he lives? Make a list of facts the class knows about the job of president.

4. Show your students a picture of George Washington. Explain that he is called the Father of Our Country. Why would someone be called that? What is the job of a "father"?

5. If you have several George Washington biographies available, share the pictures and ask the children to predict what the story will be about. What kinds of things did he do? Did he marry? Was he wealthy?

ENJOYING THE BOOK

1. Read *George Washington: A Picture Book Biography* to page 15.

2. Distribute page 20 and have students write stories about life in the Washington family. These may be placed into a class book or displayed in the classroom.

3. Ask the students to recall facts from the story about events in George Washington's life and list the events on chart paper. Have students practice reading the list.

4. Discuss the job of a surveyor. Ask students if they would like to be a surveyor. If possible, arrange for a surveyor to visit your class. Why was George Washington's work as a surveyor especially important in colonial America? Complete the survey activity on page 45.

5. Finish reading the story. Complete the list of events from George Washington's life. Ask students to illustrate one event and copy the words from the chart onto their papers. Assemble the finished pages in sequential order to make a Big Book.

6. Fill in the story web on page 23, listing things that George did for his country. Discuss why George Washington was called the "Father of Our Country."

7. Do the People and Places Word Search, page 41. If you wish, assign an original sentence to identify each person and location.

8. List the things a soldier would have needed to survive at Valley Forge. You can get ideas from the books in the reading center. Discuss the difference between needs and wants. Make a Venn diagram like the one on page 15 to compare and contrast modern needs with the needs of the colonial soldiers.

Overview of Activities *(cont.)*

ENJOYING THE BOOK *(cont.)*

9. Write a cooperative story about the war from the view point of a soldier. Ask the children to pretend that they are with Washington, fighting for freedom. Use questions like: What do they do? What do they eat? Where do they sleep? How do they feel about George Washington? Record student responses on a large sheet of poster board.

10. Provide supplies in the art center to make a Continental and British soldiers (page 24). Encourage students to vary the basic soldier with different colored hair and facial features. Display the finished soldiers as the Continental Army.

11. Make the antique paper and berry ink explained on page 44. Make several quill pens or nibs (sharpened, pencil size twigs) available and show students how to dip the pen in the ink. Thin tempera paint or fine-line black markers may be substituted for the berry ink. Use crumbled brown paper bags in place of dyed paper. Write vocabulary words, copy sentences, or write a brief story.

    To make a quill pen, use a sharp knife or razor to cut off the pointed end of a large turkey or goose feather. Cut away about ³/₄" (2 cm) from the underside of the shaft (see diagram), shaping the sides down to a point. Make a small slit in the tip end.

EXTENDING THE BOOK

1. Share other books about the life of George Washington. Ask students to give oral presentations if they wish and discuss why they liked or disliked their books. Would you like to have known a man like George Washington? Why? What would you like to ask him?

2. Make a 13-star flag like the one that Betsy Ross made for George Washington, page 57. Discuss how it is like or unlike the flag we use today.

3. Complete the activity on page 55 by coloring the map of the original 13 colonies. Use a large map or atlas to locate historic cities like Boston, Philadelphia, and Washington, D.C.

4. Print the letters G-E-O-R-G-E W-A-S-H-I-N-G-T-O-N on slips of paper. Move them around to make lots of small words. Keep a list of the words.

5. Provide information and books about other famous Americans from Washington's time. Have children complete the research activity on page 54 and present their reports to the class. Assemble the reports into a Big Book.

6. Read "Paul Revere's Ride" by Henry Wadsworth Longfellow. As a class, chart the action as the poem is read. Have students work in groups to rewrite and dramatize the story.

7. Ask children to choose a president to research for a short report. Organize the written reports sequentially in a Big Book. Report to the class about the President's part in the current events of the day.

8. Teach the children the Virginia reel and /or other simple dances from Washington's time.

What's the Story?

by

Story Strips

Finish these sentences. Cut apart the strips and glue them to the pages of a blank book. Make pictures to finish your story.

1. George Washington married _____ .

2. Martha had _____ children, Jackie and Patsy.

3. The Washingtons lived at _____ .

4. Washington was the commander in chief of the colonial

    _____ .

5. The soldiers had a hard winter at _____ .

6. America won the war, and George was elected _____ .

7. George Washington was a great leader. He listened to the people. They

    did not want to pay a new _____ .

8. George retired to Mount Vernon. He wanted to be a _____ .

Word Bank: Martha Custis, president, two, Valley Forge, Mount Vernon, army, farmer, tax

Hornbook

Books and paper were scarce in George Washington's day. Colonial children learned their ABC's and other lessons from a hornbook, a wooden frame with a printed page containing the capital and lowercase letters and a prayer. A thin layer of animal horn was placed over the page to protect it. You can make a hornbook to use for writing assignments during this unit by following these directions.

Materials: 8" x 10" (20 cm x 25 cm) brown or gray cardboard (cut from a cereal box), several copies of the writing page below, scissors, glue, one craft stick

Directions: Round off the corners of the cardboard with your scissors. Glue the writing paper to the center of the cardboard. Glue a craft stick to the back to hold like a handle. You may decorate the cardboard edge to look like wood.

Story Web

Fill in the web by listing things George Washington did for his country.

Soldier Patterns

Materials: toilet tissue tube for each pattern, copy of the patterns below, crayons, scissors, glue

Directions: Color each soldier's uniform and hat. Cut out the patterns. Glue each pattern around a tube.

Continental Soldier   British Soldier

It's the Law!

After the Revolutionary War, delegates met at Philadelphia to write the Constitution of the United States. These were to be the laws for our new country. The delegates wanted George Washington to be the president. He pledged to uphold the laws.

In the space below, write five laws that good citizens must obey or write five rules for classroom behavior. See "George Washington's Rules of Good Behavior" at the back of the book.

1. _____

_____

2. _____

_____

3. _____

_____

4. _____

_____

5. _____

_____

The Star-Spangled Banner

Illustrated by Peter Spier

Summary

Our country's national anthem was written on September 13–14, 1814, by Francis Scott Key. It commemorates the valiant defense of Fort McHenry against the bombardment by the British. This book contains words and music for four verses, as well as an illustrated evolution of the American flag from the time of the Revolution. There is also historical background on the writing of the anthem and a reproduction of Francis Scott Key's original manuscript.

The plan below suggests a schedule for using the activities in this unit. You may adapt it as you wish to your situation.

Sample Plan

Day 1

- Ask students to name some patriotic songs.
- Write a story about a time when they heard our national anthem. How did they feel?
- Locate Baltimore, Maryland, on a map.
- Read the book giving particular attention to the illustrations.
- Make a 15-star flag (page 29).
- Sing "The Star-Spangled Banner" as a class. Encourage your students to memorize the first verse.

Day 2

- Distribute copies of page 40 and ask children to learn the Pledge of Allegiance.
- Complete the worksheet How "The Star-Spangled Banner" Was Written (page 30).
- Practice the words to the anthem with the puzzle strips (page 33).
- Make a list of the national monuments in the illustrations.
- Complete the Monument Fill-in Book (pages 42–43).

Day 3

- Discuss the rules for flag display (page 31).
- Prepare and play the Monument Picture Match game (page 53).
- Read about Washington, D.C. (page 56), and make a model Washington Monument (page 39).
- Complete the Nifty Fifty math activity (page 48).
- Sing or listen to patriotic songs.
- Continue working on the Pledge of Allegiance.

Day 4

- Plan and conduct a flag ceremony.
- Write a patriotic cinquain (pages 35–36).
- Make pictures illustrating the evolution of the flag.
- Discuss other national monuments and/or places of historic significance the children have visited

Day 5

- Display the flag time line in chronological order.
- Make a personal flag (page 32).
- Make a patriotic wind sock (page 58).
- Share a snack of stars and stripes cookies and red, white, and blue gelatin dessert (page 64).

Overview of Activities

SETTING THE STAGE

1. Locate Baltimore, Maryland, on a map of the United States. This is where Francis Scott Key wrote the anthem. Is it near your state? In what direction would you go to arrive in Baltimore?

2. Brainstorm a list of patriotic songs that the students know. Focus on songs sung in music class. You may ask individuals to ask the music teacher for ideas and report back to the group.

3. Ask children to recall times when they have heard the national anthem.

4. Ask if anyone has ever visited Washington, D.C., on a vacation. If possible invite students to share photos or travel brochures from that experience. If necessary, contact a travel agency for pictures so that you will have pictures to compare with the book illustrations.

ENJOYING THE BOOK

1. Share the book with your class, taking time to explain the difficult language. It may be necessary to make a vocabulary list and look up the definitions in the dictionary. Here is a sample word list: twilight, perilous, gallantly, foe, haughty, reposes, fitfully, desolation, motto.

2. Have students write a journal entry explaining Francis Scott Key's feelings during the battle. Have them address the following question: How would you have reacted if you had been there?

3. Explain that the flag at Fort McHenry had 15 stars and 15 stripes because two states had joined the original 13 colonies in 1795. By 1818, five more states were added, and Congress decided to limit the stripes to 13 for the original colonies and add stars for new states. Read stories about the making of the first flag (see bibliography).

4. Practice the words to the first verse of "The Star-Spangled Banner." Sing the song as a group. Provide the words for the song in puzzle form (page 33). You may choose for each student to have a set of word strips and race to organize them.

5. Read the book for rhyming words: gleaming-streaming, air-there, wave-brave, beam-stream, must-just, etc. Make a class chart of these words. Encourage students to add other words that fill in the patterns.

6. Look through the book for pictures of national monuments. Make a list of them. Distribute the monument fill-in book (pages 42–43). Have students complete the pages, cut them out, and assemble them into a book.

Overview of Activities *(cont.)*

ENJOYING THE BOOK *(cont.)*

7. Discuss the rules for displaying the flag (page 31). You might also mark flag days on the calendar and learn the names for specific sections of the flag.

8. Have a parade around the classroom or school. Appoint a color guard to carry the flag and have the children march to patriotic music.

9. Learn more about our nation's capital. Complete the worksheet on page 56 and make a model of the Washington Monument (page 39).

    You may wish to show a video, *Discovering Washington, Our Nation's Capital,* (30 minutes) Film Ideas, 1988.

10. Prepare the red, white, and blue snacks (page 64) or ask students to bring them from home. It might be possible to bring in pans of red and blue gelatin and containers of whipped topping to assemble during class.

EXTENDING THE BOOK

1. Use encyclopedias and information from your reading to trace the evolution of the American flag. Assign different flags to be made by students and assemble them in chronological order for a "time line."

2. Look at flags from other countries in the encyclopedia. Which do you like the best? Why? Make a list of countries whose flags are red, white, and blue.

3. Ask your music teacher to help you teach your class the patriotic songs in their music textbooks. You may want to attend music class that day. It is important to understand that there are many songs which have a patriotic message of some kind.

4. Be sure that every student can recite the Pledge of Allegiance. Use the worksheet on page 40 and encourage everyone to earn a badge.

5. Have children design personal flags (page 32) as an exercise in self-concept. Use them as covers for collections of student work or display them for the class.

6. Make patriotic wind socks (page 58). Hang them around the classroom for a colorful decoration.

7. Research flag ceremonies. Have the children post the colors in the classroom or on the school grounds.

28

Make a 15-Star Flag

Francis Scott Key wrote "The Star Spangled Banner" in 1814. At that time the United States flag had fifteen stars and fifteen stripes. Color the flag, cut it out, and use it for a cover on a booklet containing How "The Star-Spangled Banner" Was Written (page 30), the Pledge of Allegiance (page 40), and the words to the national anthem (page 33).

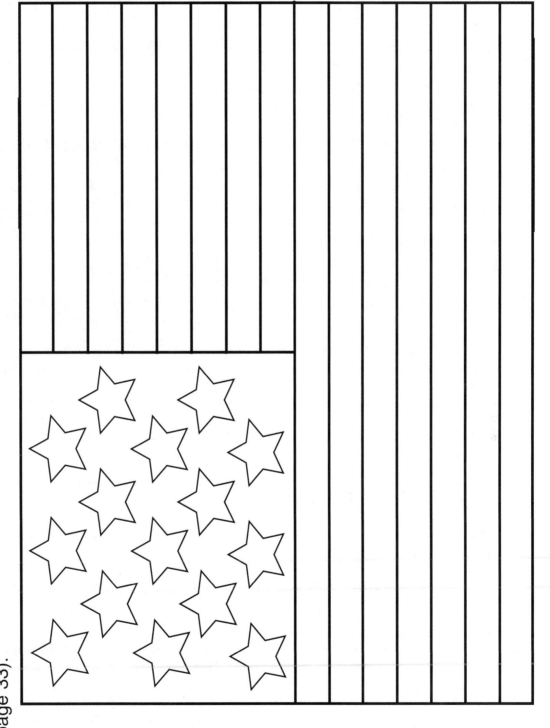

How "The Star-Spangled Banner" Was Written

In 1812 America went to war against England. The English wanted America to stop trading with the French, and they were taking sailors from American ships. The British attacked the new capitol, Washington, D.C., and burned the President's house and other buildings in 1814. When they went back to their ships, they took Dr. William Beanes as a prisoner. The British were angry because Dr. Beanes had arrested British soldiers.

President Madison sent Francis Scott Key to Baltimore to rescue Dr. Beanes. Mr. Key was a lawyer and a friend of Dr. Beanes. Key argued with the British, and they finally agreed to release Dr. Beanes, but the Americans were not allowed to return to Baltimore.

From their ship they watched as the British attacked Fort McHenry. The battle began at dawn on September 13 and continued through the night. Francis Scott Key was happy when morning came and he saw the American flag was still flying. He was a poet and wrote a poem, "The Defense of Fort McHenry," about how he felt. That poem was later set to music and called "The Star-Spangled Banner." Congress officially made "The Star-Spangled Banner" our national anthem in 1931.

Answer these questions from the information you have just read.

1. Who burned the president's house in 1814? _____

2. Why did Mr. Key go to Baltimore? _____

    _____

3. From where did Mr. Key watch the bombardment? _____

4. What was the name of the poem Mr. Key wrote? _____

5. What is our national anthem? _____

    _____

6. When did Congress officially adopt the national anthem? _____

Display of the Flag

The Continental Congress decided on June 14, 1777, that the United States flag would have 13 stripes and 13 stars, one stripe and one star for each colony. As other states joined the Union, Congress decided to keep 13 stripes for the original colonies and add a star for each new state.

Government offices and schools fly the flag every day. Many people display the flag on important national holidays: Lincoln's birthday, Washington's birthday, Independence Day, Memorial Day, Veteran's Day, and Flag Day (June 14).

The Federal Flag Code is a set of rules for displaying the flag. Here are some of those rules:

☆ The flag should not be flown outside in bad weather.

☆ The flag must never touch the ground.

☆ A flag should be flown near every school during school hours.

☆ No other flag may ever be placed above the U.S. flag.

☆ The flag may never be used in advertising of any kind.

☆ A flag in poor condition should be destroyed by burning.

☆ When the national anthem is played and a flag is displayed, all people should face the flag and salute.

☆ The flag is flown at half staff to show mourning for the death of a high ranking government official or past president.

Read the sentence and fill in the blanks.

1. The flag should not be flown o__ __ __ __ __ __ in bad weather.

2. June 14 is our national __ l __ __ day.

3. The flag must never touch the __ __ __ __ __ d.

4. The __ __ __ g Code is a set of rules for displaying the flag.

5. A flag should fly during school hours at every __ __ __ __ __ l.

6. The flag is flown at half staff to show __ o __ __ __ __ __ __ .

7. An old flag should be destroyed by __ __ r __ __ __ __ .

8. The flag has one stripe for each __ __ __ __ __ y.

Put the printed letters together in order to spell another name for the flag.

— — — — — — —

Design a Personal Flag

Look at pictures of flags of other countries, states, or organizations. Flags tell everyone something about the people they stand for. You can make a flag to tell others about yourself. Use your favorite colors to draw shapes, animals, plants, or anything that tells about you. On separate paper write a paragraph to explain why the symbols on your flag are important to you.

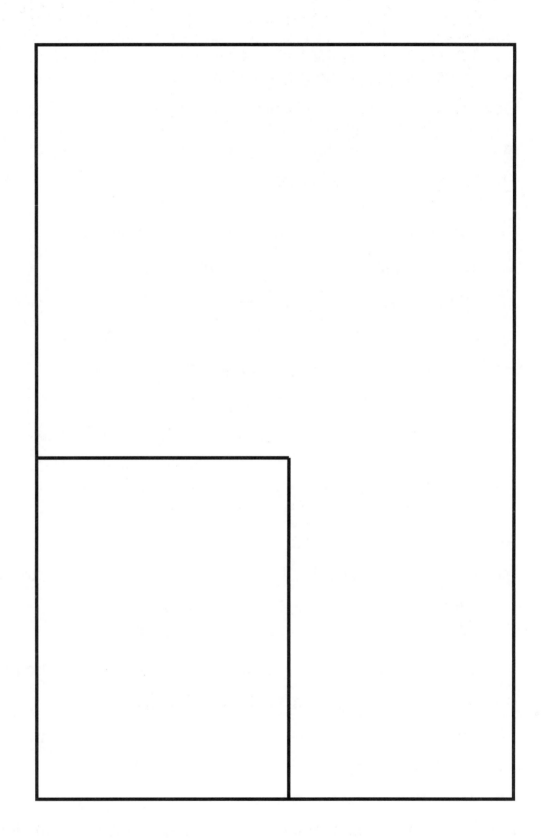

Puzzle Strips

Cut apart these strips. Mix them up and try to organize them in the correct order.

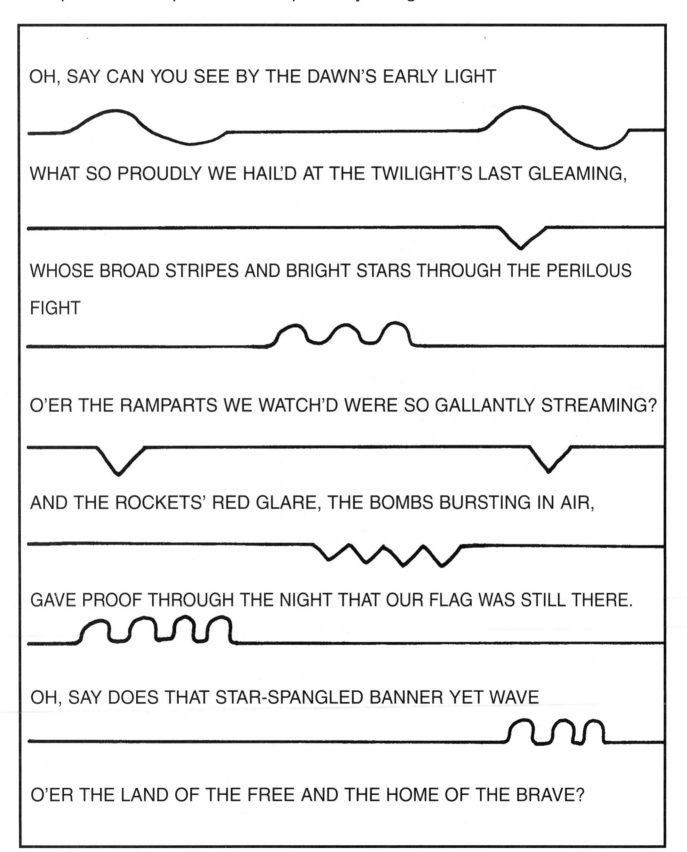

OH, SAY CAN YOU SEE BY THE DAWN'S EARLY LIGHT

WHAT SO PROUDLY WE HAIL'D AT THE TWILIGHT'S LAST GLEAMING,

WHOSE BROAD STRIPES AND BRIGHT STARS THROUGH THE PERILOUS

FIGHT

O'ER THE RAMPARTS WE WATCH'D WERE SO GALLANTLY STREAMING?

AND THE ROCKETS' RED GLARE, THE BOMBS BURSTING IN AIR,

GAVE PROOF THROUGH THE NIGHT THAT OUR FLAG WAS STILL THERE.

OH, SAY DOES THAT STAR-SPANGLED BANNER YET WAVE

O'ER THE LAND OF THE FREE AND THE HOME OF THE BRAVE?

"Over the River and Through the Wood"

This classic poem by Lydia Maria Child was first published in 1844 under the title "The Boy's Thanksgiving Day." Read the poem and circle the rhyming words.

Over the river, and through the wood,

To grandfather's house we go;

The horse knows the way

to carry the sleigh,

Through the white and drifted snow.

Over the river, and through the wood—

Oh, how the wind does blow!

It stings the toes

and bites the nose,

As over the ground we go.

Over the river and through the wood,

To have a first rate play.

Hear the bells ring,

"Ting-a-ling-ding!"

Hurrah for Thanksgiving Day!

Over the river and through the wood

Trot fast my dapple gray!

Spring over the ground

like a hunting hound!

For 'tis Thanksgiving Day.

Over the river and through the wood,

And straight through the barnyard gate.

We seem to go

extremely slow—

It is so hard to wait!

Over the river and through the wood—

Now grandmother's cap I spy!

Hurrah for the fun!

Is the pudding done?

Hurrah for the pumpkin pie!

Patriotic Poetry

Write an American Cinquain

A cinquain is a five-line poem which contains the following lines:

Line 1—one word which names the subject

Line 2—two words which describe or define the subject

Line 3—three words which express action associated with the subject

Line 4—a four-word phrase about the subject

Line 5—one word that sums up, restates, or supplies a synonym for the subject
(Sometimes it is considered a free line.)

This activity may be used to review stories and characters, to react to literature or concepts presented in class, or to introduce or review nouns, adjectives, verbs, and synonyms.

1. Read the cinquain "Stars and Stripes." Display it on the chalkboard or on a poster so that the children can refer to it as they work.

Stars and Stripes
Banner
star spangled
waving in breeze
through the long battle
Flag

2. Have children brainstorm names of people, places, or events from their reading to be used as subjects of poems. Some examples are: Pilgrims, Thanksgiving, corn, George Washington, Valley Forge, Francis Scott Key, Old Glory, Statue of Liberty, etc. List the suggestions on a piece of 12" x 18" (30 cm x 45 cm) construction paper.

3. Discuss and list as many adjectives or describing words as the children can brainstorm.

4. Make a third list containing action words to be used in lines three and four.

5. Hang all the lists in the order they will be used for the cinquain.

6. Provide students with copies of the following page and allow them to write their own cinquains about a person, event, or place. Completed poems can be read to the class, displayed, or bound into a Big Book.

My American Cinquain

Name _____

noun _____
(the subject)

adjective _____ adjective_____
(describing word) (describing word)

verb _____ verb _____ verb _____
(action word) (action word) (action word)

phrase _____ _____ _____ _____
(four words about the subject)

free line _____
(one-word summary or restatement)

Daily Writing Activities

Journals

Writing allows children to react to and internalize new knowledge. Provide children with simple books made from lined paper with red, white, or blue covers. As the unit progresses, assign appropriate topics. Here are some ideas that can be used for daily writing activities.

- Describe in detail your favorite meal.
- Tell about a trip to the grocery store.
- What do you enjoy most about the Thanksgiving holiday?
- Tell how to make popcorn. Describe what popcorn looks, tastes, and smells like.
- Choose one thing for which you are most thankful and tell why it is important to you.
- Describe a day in the army camp at Valley Forge.
- Describe George Washington's appearance.
- How would you have felt if you were with Francis Scott Key at Fort McHenry? What would you have done?
- Choose one illustration from *The Star-Spangled Banner* to describe in detail.

Paul Revere

Read "Paul Revere's Ride," by Henry Wadsworth Longfellow to the class. The poem has strong rhythm and rhyme. As the poem is read, pause to discuss the story. Ask the children to tell what has happened and record their responses on large sheets of paper. Have the children work in small groups to illustrate the pages. Collect their work in a Big Book or display the pages as a wall story.

Dramatize the story. Assign roles to students. As the story is read, either from the original or the children's retelling, have the students act it out. Older or more advanced children may write simple dialogue for their play. Present the play at the culminating activity.

Illustrate a Song

The national anthem and other patriotic songs began as poems. Read the lyrics of "America, the Beautiful" or "America." Discuss the meaning and images with the class. What was the author feeling? Do the lines rhyme? Ask the children to work in small groups to rewrite and/or illustrate each line. Compile the results in a Big Book.

Shape Book Pattern

Use this pattern to make creative writing shape books that can be used throughout the unit.

Make a Washington Monument

Follow these directions to make a model of the Washington Monument.

- Cut on the dark black lines.
- Fold on the dotted lines.
- Fold the top points in towards the center.
- Close the back and top with adhesive tape.

Stand the monument on a piece of drawing paper and add a reflecting pool.

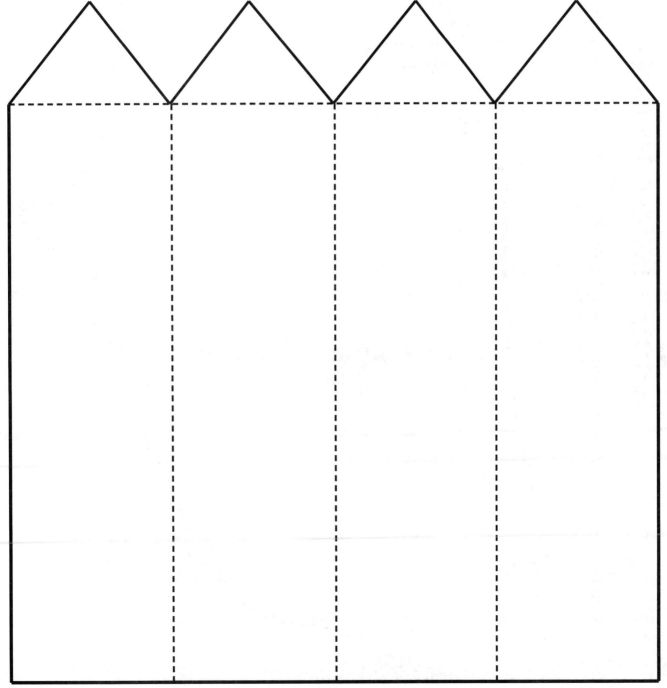

The Pledge of Allegiance

Francis Bellamy of Boston, Massachusetts, believed that American school children should make a promise of loyalty to the United States. He wrote the Pledge of Allegiance in 1892. Originally it contained the words, "my flag." Those words were changed in 1923 by the First National Flag Conference. In 1942, Congress made the pledge an official vow of loyalty to the United States. In 1954, the words "under God" were added.

Here is the Pledge of Allegiance as we say it today:

I PLEDGE ALLEGIANCE TO THE FLAG OF THE UNITED STATES OF AMERICA AND TO THE REPUBLIC FOR WHICH IT STANDS, ONE NATION UNDER GOD, INDIVISIBLE, WITH LIBERTY AND JUSTICE FOR ALL.

Can you say the Pledge from memory? When you learn it, color the badge on page 72 and wear it proudly.

People and Places Word Search

Here is a list of people and places that were important in the life of George Washington. Circle them on the puzzle.

Patsy   Martha   Lawrence

Jackie   George   Potomac

Mount Vernon   Lexington   Concord

Yorktown   Valley Forge

V A L L E Y F O R G E
O B G J Y S P M J R J
W Y M A R T H A F K T
L O O C G A P S K R C
A R U K J P U V F X M
W K N I T U P R E U V
R T T E G R O E G S X
E O V T D M T L S A W
N W E L M E O L O E K
C N R V B F M A F G T
E F N Y N C A V K O P
D R O C N O C F C S A
S R N O T G N I X E L

Monument Fill-in Book

1. The _____
   is the home of the president. It
   is the oldest public building in
   Washington, D.C.

2. The _____
   building has a large dome. It is
   the place where laws are made.

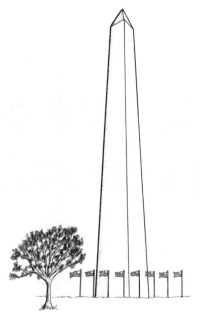

3. The _____
   is 555 feet tall. It honors our
   first president.

4. The _____
   honors the president who wrote
   the Declaration of Independence.
   It has a domed roof and columns.

Monument Fill-in Book (cont.)

5. The _____ has 36 marble columns and 56 steps. The Gettysburg Address is engraved on the wall.

6. The _____ of _____ was a gift from France. It welcomes visitors to New York harbor.

7. At the _____ _____ Memorial you can see Marines raising the U.S. flag during World War II.

My Book of Monuments

by

_____

Antique Paper and Ink

Make your own paper and ink to use for writing.

Antique Paper

Materials: a plastic washtub, water, 3–4 tea bags, plain white paper, clothesline and clothespins or layers of absorbent toweling for drying

Directions: Fill the washtub with about 3" inches (7.6 cm) of warm water. Add the tea bags and let sit for a few minutes. Carefully place the paper in the water and allow it to soak. If you wish, you may crumple the paper to create a different effect. Remove the wet paper, blot dry, and spread on absorbent towels or hang from the clothesline. When completely dry, slowly tear around the edge of the paper so that it has an uneven shape. You may use the finished product for writing important "documents" like the Bill of Rights, Constitution, or Pledge of Allegiance.

Berry Ink

Materials: ¹/₂ cup (120 mL) blueberries or strawberries, ¹/₂ tsp. (2.5 mL) salt, ¹/₂ tsp. (2.5 mL) vinegar, measuring cup and spoons, strainer, bowl, wooden spoon, small jar with tight-fitting lid

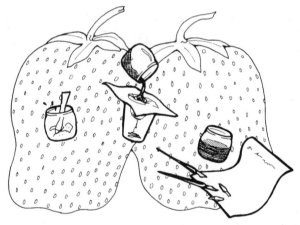

Directions: Place the berries in the strainer. Use the wooden spoon to crush the berries, collecting the juice in the bowl. Discard the fruit pulp. Stir the salt and vinegar into the juice. Pour your ink into the jar and cover tightly.

Nut Ink

Materials: 8 whole walnut shells, 1 cup (240 mL) water, ¹/₂ tsp. (2.5 mL) vinegar, ¹/₂ tsp. (2.5 mL) salt, measuring cup and spoons, strainer, saucepan, hammer, piece of cloth, small jar with tight fitting lid

Directions: Wrap the shells in the cloth. Use the hammer to crush the walnut shells. Place the crushed shells in the sauce pan with the water and bring it to a boil. Turn down the heat and simmer for ¹/₂ hour. Remove from the heat and cool and then pour through the strainer into a jar. Stir in the vinegar and salt.

(This method may also be used with birch or willow bark or roots of plants.)

Let's Survey

Surveying is the method used to make large-scale, accurate measurement. It is used for making maps and planning cities. George Washington was asked to help survey Virginia's western frontier when he was just 16 years old.

There are several ways of making measurements in a survey. Work in a small group to survey and map your classroom, using different measures.

1. Use a compass to determine the direction the classroom faces. Take turns and pace off the north/south and east/west measurements. Enter the results in the chart.

2. Compare the results. Are the number of paces the same?

3. Now, measure the classroom using a metal tape with standard measurements (feet or meters) and enter the results on the chart.

4. Which measurement is more accurate? Which would you use for making a map?

Names	Tape Measurements	
	North/South	East/West

5. Use one set of measurements to make a boundary map of the classroom

Extension: Use a second kind of standard measure and compare the results. Which is the bigger number, meters or feet?

Graph and Count Coins

Materials:

- four small, wide-mouthed containers or jar
- coins, ten each of pennies, nickels, dimes, and quarters (Use play money or duplicate page 78 and cut apart the coins.)
- a permanent black marker

To prepare the jars: Use the marker to label the jars: quarters, dimes, nickels, and pennies. Place the coins in the appropriate jars.

Directions: Reach into the jar labeled quarters and grab as many coins as you can. Count how many you have and write the number on the graph. Do the same with the other jars.

Coin	Number of Coins Grabbed									
Pennies										
Nickels										
Dimes										
Quarters										
	1	2	3	4	5	6	7	8	9	10

Which coin on the graph has the most? _____

Which coin on the graph has the fewest? _____

Are any the same? Which coins? _____

Lucky 13

The United States began as a group of 13 colonies. The flag George Washington designed had 13 stars, one for each colony, arranged in a circle. It looked like the picture below.

Complete the number sentences on the flag below. If the missing number is even (2,4,6,8,10), color the stripe red. If it is odd (1,3,5,7,9,11), do not color the stripe.

1. ____ + 7 = 13

2. 10 + ____ = 13

3. 5 + ____ = 13

4. ____ + 12 = 13

5. 9 + ____ = 13

6. 2 + ____ = 13

7. ____ + 4 + 1 = 13

8. 13 − ____ = 6

9. 13 − ____ = 5

10. 13 − 4 = ____

11. 13 − 9 = ____

12. 13 − 2 = ____

13. 13 − ____ = 1

How many red stripes are there? _____ How many are white? _____

Challenge: Get 13 stars (page 78). Arrange them in an organized pattern. Draw your best pattern on the flag, and color the field blue.

Nifty Fifty

Today America is made up of fifty individual states. There are 50 stars on the flag.

Can you count to 50 by twos? Fill in the missing numbers.

2, 4, 6, ___ , 10, 12, ___ , 16, 18,___ , 22, ___ , 26, 28, 30, ___ , 34, 36, ___ , ___ , 42, 44, ___ , 48, ___

Can you count to 50 by fives? Fill in the missing numbers.

5, 10, ___ , 20, ___ , ___ , 35, 40, 45, ___

Can you count to 50 by tens? Fill in the missing numbers.

10, ___ , 30, ___ , 50

Here are some math problems that equal fifty. Fill in the missing numbers.

1. 34 +___ = 50   4. 13 +___ = 50   7. 75 −___ = 50

2. 27 +___ = 50   5. 42 +___ = 50   8. 83 −___ = 50

3. 18 +___ = 50   6. 39 +___ = 50   9. 59 −___ = 50

Extension: Copy 50 stars. Cut them apart and sort into groups of twos, fives, or tens for counting. Use the stars as a manipulative to help solve problems.

Make a Compass

Experiment 1

A compass is used to find directions. It is really a magnet that is attracted to the north and south magnetic poles of the earth. The Pilgrims used a compass when they traveled from England to America.

Materials: a sewing needle, a bar magnet, a cork, a pan of water, a common compass

Directions: Rub the needle on the bar magnet to magnetize it. Rest the needle on the cork.

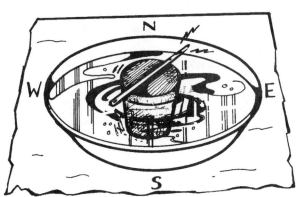

Float the cork on the surface of the water. The needle will point in one direction.

Check the common compass to see if your compass is pointing in the same direction. In what direction is the compass pointing?

Experiment 2

Here is another experiment using a magnet to show direction:

Materials: a bar magnet, about 24 inches (61 cm) of string, a 20-inch (51 cm) square of paper, a marker

Directions: Tie one end of the string securely around the bar magnet. Fasten the other end of the string to a table top.

Allow the magnet to swing free until it stops moving. Mark the end pointing north with an N and the opposite end (south) with an S. Draw a circle on the paper and divide it into fourths. Mark the ends of the lines with N,S,E,W (north, south, east, and west) like the face of a compass. Place the paper on the floor, lining up the N-S line with the direction of the bar magnet.

On the back of this page, describe what you see to the north, south, east, west. Explain the directions northeast, northwest, southeast, and southwest.

Planting Corn

The Pilgrims planted many crops in their new home with the help of friendly Indians like Squanto and Samoset. The Indians knew that corn would grow better if a small fish was dropped into the hole with the seeds. The fish was fertilizer. Indians and colonists planted five seeds in each hill to be sure that at least one plant would grow. The colonists made up a rhyme about planting corn:

> One for the blackbird, one for the crow,
> One for the cutworm, and two to grow.

Try the following activity to learn if fish help corn to grow.

Materials: corn seeds, soil, 2 foil pans, small fish (available at a bait store) or fish meal fertilizer, trowel for digging

Directions: Fill each pan with soil. Use the trowel to make several hills of soil in each pan. In one pan, place a small fish in each hill, add five seeds, and cover with soil. Plant seeds in the other pan without fish. Water both pans and place them in a sunny window. Water the pans when the soil is dry.

Make a chart on the chalkboard or on poster board. Record the planting date. Observe the corn plants. When the plants sprout, record the date. Compare the results. Continue to water the plants and measure and compare their growth at regular intervals. Discuss these questions in class: Which seeds grew faster? Why do you think this happened?

Extensions:

- Indians taught colonists to plant other crops in the valleys between the corn hills. Corn stalks supported bean plants, and squash or pumpkin leaves shaded the roots, so everything grew better. Add these plants to your garden.

- Make a classroom display of several varieties of corn, such as Indian corn, sweet corn, field corn. Compare them and write descriptions of each.

- Plant seeds in foam cups. Keep a log, writing or drawing pictures to record the growth of the fertilized and non-fertilized plants.

- Serve a treat of popped corn.

The Sense of Taste

"Tea Party"

England wanted the colonists to pay a tax on tea. The colonists refused to pay the tax. On December 16, 1773, a group of colonists dressed as Indians dumped the tea into Boston Harbor.

Today many types and flavors of tea are available. Tea is called an infusion because it is the result of soaking a solid, leaves, in a liquid, water. This gives the water the flavor of the leaves, but the leaves do not dissolve. It is possible to prepare drinks similar to tea by adding spices to boiling water. Prepare several infusions for tasting and decide on some words to describe them. Write your ideas on the lines below.

Materials:

- several teaspoons
- tea ball or strainer
- a variety of flavored tea bags
- a variety of whole herbs and/or spices: anise, cinnamon, allspice, nutmeg, mint, oregano, sage, cloves, basil, rosemary

- tea kettle
- boiling water
- cups
- sugar or honey

Directions: Pour boiling water into a cup over a tea bag or tea ball holding about 1/4 teaspoon (1.25 mL) of spices. Allow to steep (soak) for about three minutes. Remove the tea bag or ball and taste. Add sweetener if desired. Think of words that describe the taste. Here are some suggestions: sweet, bitter, tangy, sour, tart, weak, strong.

Note to teacher: Ground spices will dissolve in water. Using them will produce a variety of flavors, but that is not an "infusion."

Infusion	How It Tastes
_____	_____
_____	_____
_____	_____
_____	_____

Taste Without Smell

Have you ever noticed that food does not taste as good when you have a cold? Here is an experiment to prove how important the sense of smell is to taste.

Materials:

- peeled apple
- peeled orange
- peeled onion
- peeled potato
- grater

- blindfold
- four plates and forks
- clip clothespins (for the nose)
- glass of water and basin

Directions:

1. Grate the apple, potato, onion, and orange. Place them into four separate plates.
2. Blindfold one of your classmates. He or she will be the food taster. Clip his or her nose shut.
3. Put a small amount of one of the foods onto his or her tongue.
4. Have the taster roll the food around in his or her mouth without chewing or swallowing it.
5. Ask the taster to guess what the food is. Record his or her guess on the chart below.
6. Repeat steps 3 through 5 with the other foods. Have the taster rinse his or her mouth with water after each food tasting.

Try this experiment with another classmate (Taster 2). Record the results in the chart.

Taster	What was your guess?			
	Apple	Potato	Onion	Orange
1				
2				

Extension: Compare other foods that come in different flavors, like chocolate/vanilla ice cream, sodas, etc., using the same method.

Monument Picture Match

Draw a line to match the picture to its name.

Jefferson Memorial

Washington Monument

White House

Lincoln Memorial

Capitol

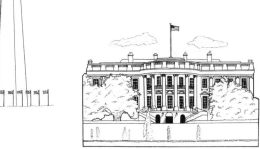

Iwo Jima Memorial

Statue of Liberty

Note to teacher: You may cut apart the pictures and name labels, glue them to index cards, and use them as a concentration-style matching game.

Famous American Research

Here are the names of more famous people from the early days of America:

Benjamin Franklin	**William Penn**	**John Hancock**
Betsy Ross	**Peter Stuyvestant**	**Samuel Adams**
William Bradford	**Paul Revere**	**Pocahontas**
Captain John Smith	**Ethan Allen**	**Squanto**

Pick one that you would like to know more about. Read a book about that person or use an encyclopedia. Answer these questions and share the information with the class.

Name _____

Date of birth _____

Parents' names _____

Country and/or state where he/she was born _____

Interesting fact from his/her childhood_____

_____

_____

_____

Job or career _____

Important contribution to history _____

_____

_____

_____

Thirteen Original Colonies

Here is the way the country looked when George Washington was president. Read the names of the colonies. Follow the directions and answer the questions below.

1. Which colony is farthest north? _____

2. Which colony is the farthest south? _____

3. Color Virginia blue.

4. Color New York red.

5. Which colony is the smallest? _____

Washington, D.C.

When George Washington was president, Congress met in several different cities, including Philadelphia, Boston, and New York. In 1790, Congress appointed a committee to choose a permanent location for the capital. It was decided that a new city should be built and that it should not be part of any state. Maryland and Virginia gave land for the new city on the Potomac River. It is known as the District of Columbia.

The planners decided that the Capitol building should be on a hill overlooking the city because it was the most important building. On September 18, 1793, George Washington laid the cornerstone of the capitol building. Washington died before any of the buildings in the new city were completed. It was named in his honor. John Adams was the first president to live in the president's house, and Thomas Jefferson was the first president to take office in Washington in 1801.

Washington was not a good place to live in those early years. The city was dirty, and the streets were unpaved. There was a swamp full of mosquitos that caused disease. Many people became ill. They thought that Washington, D.C., would never become a great city.

During the War of 1812, the British stormed Washington and burned the Capitol, the president's house, and other public buildings. When the president's house was rebuilt, it was painted white. Since then it has been called the White House.

Today there are many buildings, museums, and historic monuments in Washington, D.C.

Find the following facts about our capital.

1. Our capital is not in any of the states. It is located in an area called_____

2. Our capital was named for our first president, _____

3. The first president to live in Washington, D.C., was _____

4. The first president to take office in Washington was _____

5. The most important building in Washington is the _____

6. The president's house is called the_____

Make a 13-Star Flag

This is the flag that George Washington designed for the new country. The thirteen stars stand for the thirteen original colonies. Follow these directions to finish the flag:

- Make a star on each dot.
- Read the words and color the flag.
- Cut out your flag and tape or staple it to a plastic straw.

Blue

Red

Red

Red

Red

Red

Red

Red

Patriotic Wind Sock

Make a patriotic wind sock using the materials and directions below. When you are done, hang your wind sock in the classroom or at home.

Materials:

- red and white crepe paper streamers
- blue construction paper 9 x 18 inches (23 x 46 cm)
- glue, stapler, scissors, adhesive tape
- white chalk or silver glitter
- yarn or string

Directions:

1. Use the white chalk to make stars on one side of the blue paper. (If you wish, make the stars with silver glitter.)
2. Form the blue construction paper into a cylinder.
3. Glue closed along the shorter side. Staple to ensure stability.
4. Attach red and white streamers to one end with glue.
5. Cut three 12-inch (30.5 cm) lengths of string. Tape them about 6 inches (15 cm) apart to the top of the blue construction paper.
6. Knot the three strings together to make a hanger.

Pilgrim Hats

Have students make the pilgram hats and collars below. Use them with the culminating activities.

══ Boy's Hat ══

Materials: 6" x 18" (15 cm x 46 cm) and 9" x 12" (23 cm x 30 cm) gray construction paper, 2" x 18" (5 cm x 46 cm) black construction paper, scissors, glue, stapler

Directions: Cut the hat brim (page 60) from the 9" x 12" (23 cm x 30 cm) gray paper. Glue the black strip to the long side of the 6" x 18" (15 cm x 46 cm) gray paper and tape the 6" (15 cm) sides together to form the crown. Fold up the tabs on the brim and glue the crown in place.

══ Girl's Bonnet ══

Materials: 2" x 15" (5 cm x 38 cm) white tagboard, 12" x 20" (30 cm x 51 cm) white tissue paper, glue stick, scissors, stapler, 36" (91 cm) of white ribbon or yarn, hat band pattern (page 60)

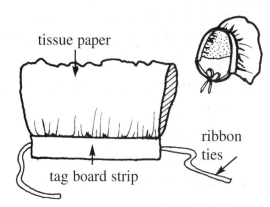

tissue paper

ribbon ties

tag board strip

Directions: Cut the ends of the tagboard strip as shown. Glue the tissue paper along the edge of the strip, gathering in the excess length. Allow to dry. Gently fold the tissue in half (right sides together) and glue the back of the bonnet closed. If desired for fit, glue or tape two tucks on the back neck edge. Staple half the ribbon to each end of the front band to tie under the chin.

══ Collar ══

Materials: 12" x 18" (30 cm x 46 cm) each of gray and white paper (gray for boy's collar, white for girl's collar), scissors

Directions: Follow the diagram to create collars.

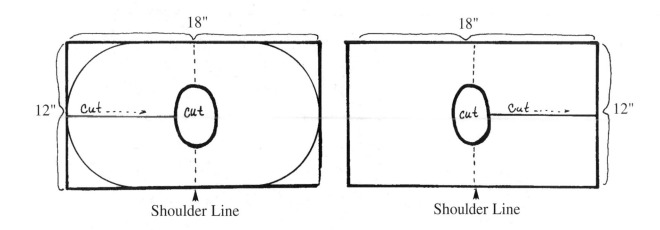

Pilgrim Hats *(cont.)*

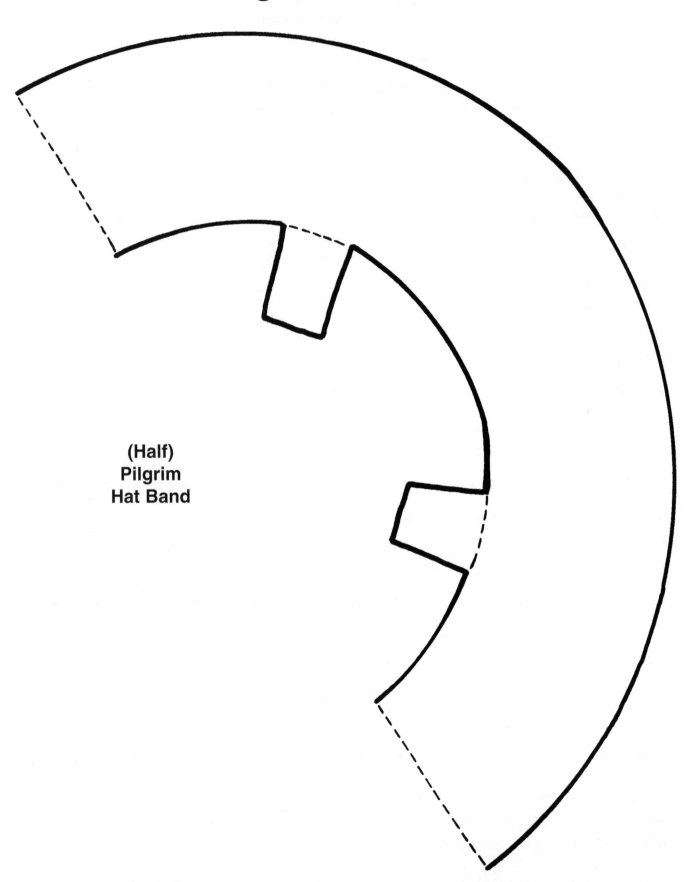

**(Half)
Pilgrim
Hat Band**

Colonial Toys

Materials: dried corn husks, pan or basin of water, scissors, string (or twist ties), markers

Cornhusk Dolls

Directions: Soak the husks in water to make them pliable. Choose four large husks. Join them together with string or a twist tie (covered wire) about 2" (5 cm) from the top. Wrap short strips of husk (or paper) around the top two inches (5 cm) to form a tight ball. This will be the head. Flip the long husks over the ball and tie a string around the neck to hold the head in place. Choose two shorter husks to use for arms. Tie off each end to make hands. Insert them under the neck. Use string to tie off the waistline. Fluff the bottom portion out to make the skirt or cut the bottom up the middle and tie off two feet for a boy doll in pants.

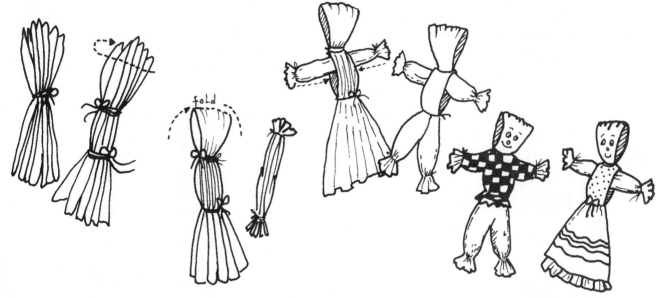

Humming Toy

Materials: heavy cardboard, scissors, markers, hole punch, string

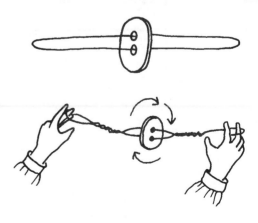

Directions: Cut a three-inch (7.6 cm) circle from the cardboard. Punch two holes in the circle. Decorate the circle with the markers. Cut 36" (91 cm) of string. Insert the string through the holes and tie. Hold the ends of the string between your hands and turn the circle until the string is tightly wound. As you pull the string, the toy will unwind and make a humming sound.

Design a Sampler

In colonial times little girls made samplers as a way to practice their sewing and learn their letters and numbers. It was a picture of an alphabet and numbers with a colorful border of flowers, houses, hearts, or people. At the bottom it had the name of the person who made it and the date it was finished. Many families framed samplers and hung them like pictures.

Follow the directions below to design your own sampler.

1. Make a small x on each of the dots to finish the letters and numbers. If you prefer, you may connect the dots to reveal the letters/numbers.

2. Design a colorful border. Be sure to sign your name and the date on the bottom.

3. Take your sampler home and hang it up!

Music in Colonial Life

The colonists did not have radios, television, or movies for entertainment. They did have music and used it in different ways.

━━━━━ Telling Time with Music ━━━━━

Today we rely on clocks and timers to tell us when something is done. Most colonial families did not have clocks. One way to time the cooking of things like eggs was by singing a certain hymn or song. When the song was done, so was the food!

Try This: Choose a song everyone knows. Sing it as a class and time how long it takes to sing one verse. How long for the whole song? When would this be useful in our world?

━━━━━ Music Goes to War ━━━━━

In England and other countries, soldiers marched to music when they went to battle. "Yankee Doodle" is, perhaps, the oldest "American" song. It was originally written by an Englishman to make fun of colonists because they were not good soldiers.

During the Revolutionary War, the colonists adopted it as their own. Imagine how the British felt when they had to march to "Yankee Doodle" as they surrendered at Yorktown!

Try This: Form a line and march around the classroom. Then add some music, like "Yankee Doodle," or a rousing patriotic march by John Phillip Sousa. Was it easier to march with or without the music? Select some music for use in a flag ceremony or parade with the flag.

━━━━━ Music as Entertainment ━━━━━

As the colonies grew, many people came from different places. They brought their music and dances with them. Jigs and reels were two popular forms of dance.

Try This: Learn to do the Virginia reel. Present your dance at the culminating activity.

Colonial Cooking

▬▬▬▬ Red, White, and Blue Gelatin Dessert ▬▬▬▬

Ingredients:

- two 6 oz. (170 g) packages of red gelatin
- two 6 oz. (170 g) packages of blue gelatin
- water
- whipped dessert topping
- clear plastic cups and spoons

Directions: Prepare the gelatin according to package directions. After it is set layer it into the plastic cups with the whipped topping.

▬▬▬▬ Stars and Stripes Cookies ▬▬▬▬

Ingredients:

- 20 oz. (576 g) refrigerated sugar cookie dough
- star-shaped cookie cutter
- confectioner's sugar
- milk
- red and blue decorating sugar

Directions: Roll out the cookie dough according to package directions. Cut into star shapes and bake as directed. Prepare a thin icing from confectioner's sugar thinned with a little milk. Ice the cooled cookies and decorate with stripes of red and blue sugar.

▬▬▬▬ Rhode Island Jonny Cake ▬▬▬▬

Ingredients:

- 2 cups (480 mL) white corn meal
- 2 tablespoons (30 mL) sugar
- 2¼ teaspoons (11 mL) salt
- 2 cups (480 mL) milk.
- electric griddle or skillet

Directions: Mix dry ingredients in a bowl. Make a well in the center and pour in the milk. Beat until smooth and well mixed. Preheat the skillet. It is hot enough when drops of water sprinkled on it dance in small beads. Lightly grease the griddle or skillet. Drop batter by tablespoonfuls onto the heated griddle or skillet. Cook until browned on one side; turn with a spatula and brown the other side. Serve hot with butter and maple syrup.

▬▬▬▬ Quick Vegetable Soup (for 12) ▬▬▬▬

Ingredients:

- 1 46 oz.(1.36 L) can tomato juice
- 1 16 oz.(454 g) can stewed tomatoes
- 2 10 oz.(280 g) packages of frozen mixed vegetables
- 3–5 beef and/or chicken bouillon cubes
- water
- a crock pot, serving ladle, can opener, foam cups and plastic spoon

Directions: Gather the students early in the morning to prepare the soup. Combine all ingredients in the crock pot and add water to fill. Stir to mix and cook (on high) for about two hours. Reduce to low heat when the vegetables are soft. Serve in foam cups.

Colonial Games

In Virginia and other colonies, people participated in many games and foot races. Other popular activities were jousting, swimming contests, and canoe races. In cold weather skating, sledding, and forms of hockey were favorite pastimes.

Here are some colonial games you can enjoy with your class:

"Bowls" — This game is like bowling without pins where the players roll balls to hit a target.

Cat's Cradle — This is a game that needs two players and about two feet (61 cm) of string knotted together on the ends.

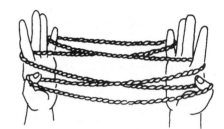

Share the book *Cat's Cradle: A Book of String Figures* by Anne Akers Johnson, Klutz Press, 1993, for directions on playing the string game.

Checkers — Called "draughts" by the colonists, you may play regular rules for checkers using corn for playing pieces.

Fox and Geese — To play this version of tag, draw a very large chalk circle on the ground. Add a center circle, and spokes like a wheel. The fox is "it." He chases the geese around the circle trying to tag them. The geese are safe in the center circle. As the geese are caught, they become "it" and chase all the others.

Hoop and Stick — A hoop and stick were favorite toys. Children practiced rolling a large hoop downhill, using only a stick. Another game for two players involved tossing a hoop from two crossed sticks. The receiving player caught the hoop on one stick.

Hopscotch — Played by similar rules as today, it was also called "Scotch Hoppers".

Jackstones — This is the same as the modern game of jacks, using jacks made of pebbles or pieces of metal.

Jump Rope — Children enjoyed skipping to a familiar rhyme like "Ring Around the Rosy" or "London Bridge."

Marbles — "Ringers" was a popular game with colonial children. One player places his marbles inside a large chalk circle drawn on the ground. The player shoots one of his marbles into the ring, attempting to move the opponents' marbles. The score is determined by how many of the opponent's marbles you shoot out of the ring.

Quoits — This game is like ring toss or horseshoes, where rings are tossed at a stake.

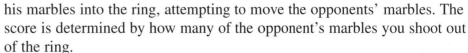

Colonial Children's Day

To celebrate the successful end of the unit, give the children a first-hand experience in colonial living. Use some or all of these ideas to have a special Colonial children's day.

Encourage your students to dress in period clothing and be prepared to take photographs of them enjoying themselves.

- Ask parents to assist in the activities. Have them dress in period clothing, too!
- Invite parents and/or guests to enjoy the day (or the lunch activity), using the pop-up card on page 12 to make invitations.
- Set up four areas of the classroom for activities. Each center addresses a different aspect of colonial life.
- Allow enough time (about 2 hours) for all students to work through the centers.
- Have at least one parent volunteer for each area.
- As part of the experience, have children help to prepare a simple lunch.

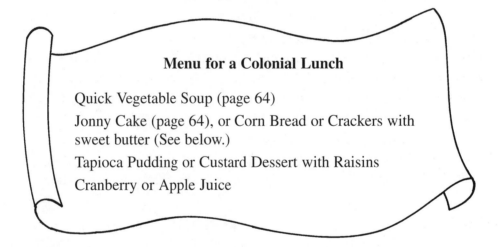

Menu for a Colonial Lunch

Quick Vegetable Soup (page 64)

Jonny Cake (page 64), or Corn Bread or Crackers with sweet butter (See below.)

Tapioca Pudding or Custard Dessert with Raisins

Cranberry or Apple Juice

Centers

Home

Decorate the area with a window and clapboard wall. Include a rocking chair for the parent and a paper fireplace. Children will sit on the floor.

Activities: Complete the sampler (page 62). You may wish to provide fabric, needles, floss, and embroidery hoops for children to experiment with actual stitching. Prepare and serve the colonial lunch.

School

Place near a chalkboard for writing and copying. Arrange the desks in straight rows.

Activities: Copy classroom rules, handwriting, or math facts from the board. Make hornbooks (page 22) and use quill pens and berry ink (page 44) for the written work. Students should sit straight and respond politely. They should stand to recite if reading aloud.

Colonial Children's Day *(cont.)*

Centers *(cont.)*

Chores

Have foam cups, soil, seeds, and digging implements available. If students are making butter, you will need clean glass mayonnaise jars, heavy cream, a slotted spoon, and a dish.

Activities: Plant corn, beans, and/or pumpkin seeds in individual foam cups. Observe and tend the "garden."

Churning Butter

Churn butter. It was common for colonial children to help with this weekly chore. Have each student shake the jar vigorouly a specific number of times or time each child's turn the colonial way, by singing! (See page 63.)

Materials: Clean glass jar, like a mayonnaise jar, $^1/_2$ pint (240 mL) heavy cream.

Directions: Allow cream to sit at room temperature for about an hour. Pour the cream into the glass jar. Shake the jar until butter begins to form (about 25 minutes). Remove the solid butter and wash it under cold running water. Pack in a dish.

Play

Provide an area with no furniture or have the parent helper take children outside. Make materials available for some or all of the games listed on page 65.

Activities: Make a variety of games (page 65) available for free play.

After lunch has been served, allow time for students to share their learning by presenting puppet shows, plays, and songs they have learned. Demonstrate a flag ceremony, march in a parade, and/or dance the Virginia reel.

Parent Letter

_____
(date)

Dear Parents,

We will soon be starting a whole-language thematic unit about our country. Please help us by permitting your child to bring items related to colonial or revolutionary America. Flags, Thanksgiving pictures or articles, travel brochures about Washington, D.C., and/or national monuments will enrich our unit.

Our unit will culminate with a Colonial Children's Day on _____ . We would like the students to dress as colonists for this experience. Girls might wear long skirts, aprons, and shawls. Dark short pants, white shirts, and knee socks are appropriate for the boys. This activity will include a simple, early-American lunch to be prepared in the classroom. We will need the following items in order to prepare our lunch:

- **46 oz. (1.36 L) cans of tomato juice**
- **16 oz. (454 g) cans of stewed tomatoes**
- **10 oz. (238 g) packages of frozen mixed**
- **vegetables**
- **beef and/or chicken bouillon cubes**
- **white corn meal**
- **apple or cranberry juice**

- **tapioca or custard pudding**
- **foam cups**
- **plastic tableware**
- **corn for popping**
- **red, white, and blue gelatin**
- **stars and stripes sugar cookies**

If you can supply any of these items or are available to help in the classroom for the culminating activity, please fill out and return the note below.

Thank you,

_____
(teacher)

·· (cut) ··

❏ Yes, I can help with the activities.

I can provide _____ .

Please call me at _____ to make arrangements.

The best time to call me is _____ .

Name _____

Book Report Form

Name _____

Title _____

Author_____

Summarize the most important event from the story _____

_____

_____

_____

_____

My favorite character was _____ because_____

_____

_____

_____

Why is this book important to the theme, "My Country"?_____

_____

_____

Would you recommend this book to a friend? Tell why or why not. _____

_____

_____

_____

Reading Record

Each student should make a turkey body as a base for an individual reading record. Cut as many turkey head/neck patterns and feathers as needed. Staple them to paper plates as shown, adding feathers as needed. For each book read about the theme, a feather will be added to the turkey. Print the book title on the feather and glue in place. The turkeys may be displayed at student desks or in the reading area.

This pattern may also be used for other activities:

- Print one word from a sentence on each feather. Students read and glue them in order on the turkey.

- Designate one turkey "nouns" and another "verbs." Prepare a group of feathers with words to be sorted to the correct turkey.

- Make one turkey body and five feathers for each student. Have them write each line of their cinquain on a feather and glue them in sequential order to the body.

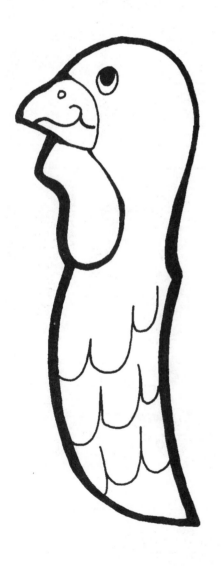

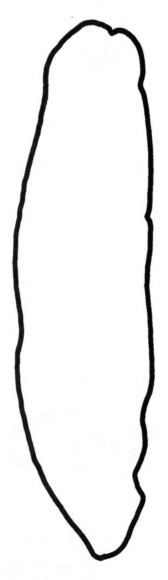

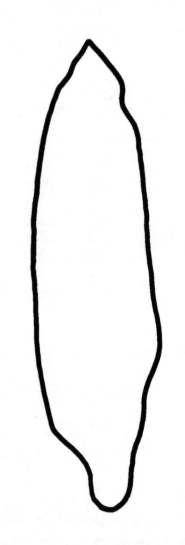

Bookmarks

Words to Learn

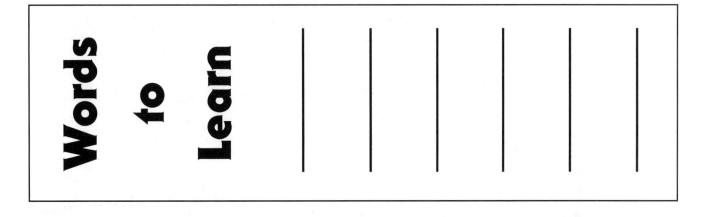

I'm thankful I can read.

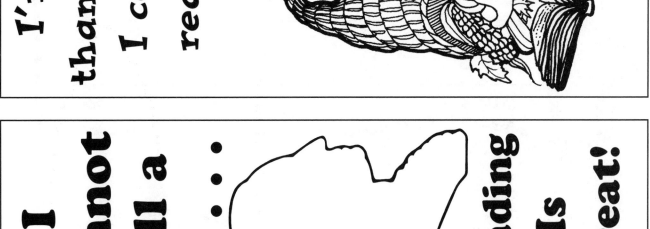

I cannot tell a lie . . .

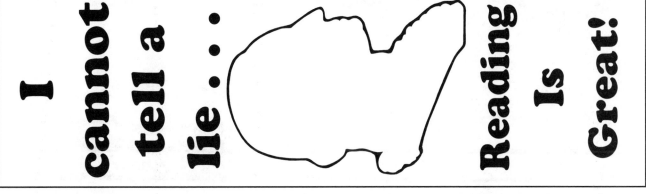

Reading Is Great!

All-American Reader

Incentives

I can say the first verse of

"The Star-Spangled Banner"

☆ ☆ ☆ ☆ ☆

Congratulations to

_____

_____   _____
Date   **Teacher**

is awarded this
GOOD CITIZEN
badge for _____

Yes!
I can say the
Pledge . . .
Ask me.

Patriotic Game

Materials: patriotic game board (pages 74–75), stars (page 78), true/false Cards (below), game markers, die or spinner

Directions: Duplicate and laminate the game board, stars, and true/false cards. Prepare an answer key for the cards. (See page 80 for answers.)

To Play: Decide which player will go first. The first player rolls the die and moves his marker the designated number of spaces. If the marker lands on a question mark, the player draws and responds to a true or false card and collects a star for a correct answer. The game progresses in this manner until both players reach the White House. The player with the most stars at the end is the winner.

1. George Washington is called the Father of his country.	7. Fort McHenry is in Baltimore, Maryland.	13. The Pilgrims came in a ship called the *Santa Maria*.
2. George and Martha Washington had five children.	8. Francis Scott Key went to Ft. McHenry to rescue his friend.	14. The Indians helped the Pilgrims plant corn.
3. George and Martha Washington lived at Mount Vernon.	9. There were 13 stars and stripes on the first American flag.	15. The leader of the Pilgrims was Governor Bradford.
4. George Washington's first wife was Annabelle Jones.	10. The flag should never touch the ground.	16. The Pilgrims had cranberries at the first Thanksgiving.
5. The colonial army had a pleasant summer at Valley Forge.	11. When a flag is old, it is OK to throw it in the trash.	17. Indians taught the Pilgrims about corn.
6. Washington, D.C., is the capital of America.	12. The Pilgrims sailed to America in 1620.	18. Our national anthem is "The Star-Spangled Banner."

Game Board

74

Game Board (cont.)

Bulletin Board

This bulletin board may be used to display a variety of students' written work or pictures appropriate to this unit. The board may be titled: **We Are Thankful, We Love America,** or **We Are Good Citizens.** Enlarge a map of the United States to use in the center of the board. Decorate the country with red and white stripes and stars. Make large copies of the patterns below and on page 77. Use them to frame student work or lists of vocabulary words, Pledge of Allegiance, or words of "The Star-Spangled Banner."

Patterns (1 of 7)

Bulletin Board *(cont.)*

Patterns*(cont.)*

Star and Coin Patterns

Duplicate and laminate these patterns to use as manipulatives or game pieces.

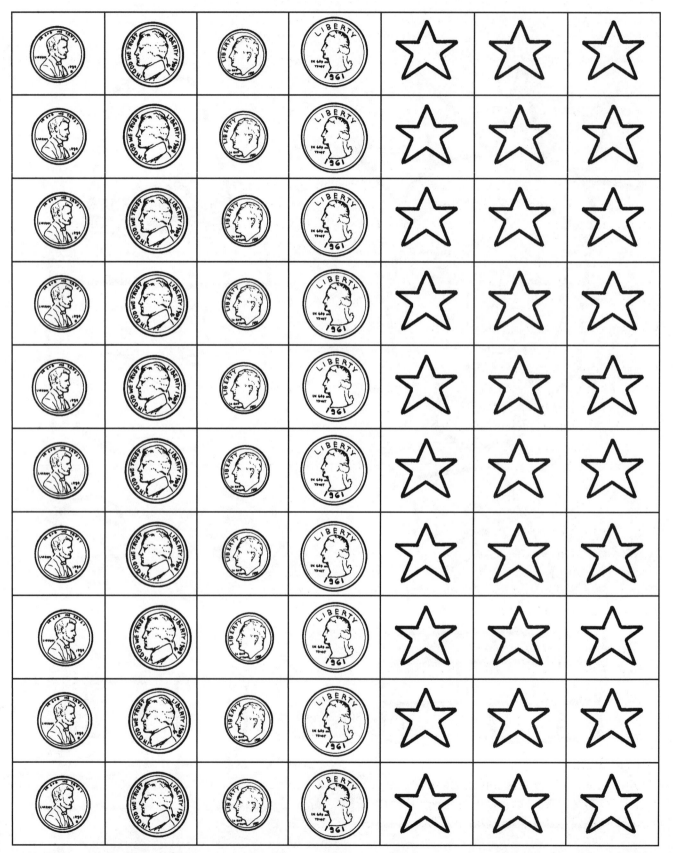

Bibliography

Colonial Times

Accorsi, William. *Friendship's First Thanksgiving.* Holiday House, 1992

Bauer, Caroline Feller. *Thanksgiving Stories and Poems.* Harper Collins, 1994

Bernstein, Rebecca Sample. *Felicity's Craft Book.* Pleasant Company Publishing, 1994

Celsi, Teresa Noel. *Squanto and the First Thanksgiving.* Raintree, 1989

Child, Lydia Maria. *Over the River and Through The Wood.* Coward, McCann and Geoghegan, Inc. 1974

dePaola, Tomie. *An Early American Christmas.* Holiday House, 1987

Felicity's Cook Book: A Peek at Dining in the Past with Meals You Can Cook Today. Pleasant Company Publishing, 1994

George, Jean Craighead. *The First Thanksgiving.* Philomel, 1993

Gibbons, Gail. *Thanksgiving Day.* Holiday House, 1983

Greene, Carol. *Pocahontas: Daughter of a Chief.* Childrens Press, 1988

Lizon, Karen Helene. *Colonial American Holidays and Entertainment.* Watts, 1993

Loeper, John J. *The Shop on High Street—The Toys and Games of Early America.* Atheneum, 1974

Tripp, Valerie. *Felicity Learns a Lesson.* Pleasant Company Publishing, 1991

Tripp, Valerie. *Felicity Saves the Day.* Pleasant Company Publishing, 1991

Waters, Kate. *Samuel Eaton's Day: A Day in the Life of a Pilgrim Boy.* Scholastic, 1993

Waters, Kate. *Sarah Morton's Day: A Day in the Life of a Pilgrim Girl.* Scholastic, 1993

George Washington and the Revolution

Adler, David A. *A Picture Book of George Washington.* Holiday House, 1989

Chant, Christopher. *Presidents of the United States.* Gallery Books, 1990

Clark, Philip, and Marshall Cavendish. *The American Revolution.* 1988

Fisher, Aileen. *My First Presidents' Day Book* (poetry). Childrens Press, 1987

Fritz, Jean. *Will You Sign Here, John Hancock?* General, 1976

Jacobs, William Jay. *Washington.* Macmillan, 1991

Longfellow, Henry Wadsworth. *Paul Revere's Ride.* Dutton, 1990

Marzollo, Jean. *In 1776.* Scholastic, 1994

Small, David. *George Washington's Cows.* Farrar, Straus and Giroux, 1994

Flags and Monuments

A Kid's Guide to Washington, D.C., Harcourt, Brace, Jovanovich, 1989

Fisher, Leonard Everett. *Stars and Stripes.* Holiday House, 1993

Fradin, Dennis B. *The Flag of the United States.* Childrens Press, 1988

Maestro, Betsy and Guilio. *The Story of the Statue of Liberty.* Lothrop, Lee, Shepard, 1986

Razzi, James. *Star-Spangled Fun!* Parents' Magazine Press, 1976

Turck, Mary. *Washington, D.C.* Crestwood House, 1989

Waters, Kate. *The Story of the White House.* Scholastic, 1991

Poetry and Music

Bates, Katharine Lee. *America the Beautiful* (song). Atheneum, 1993

Little, Lessie Jones. *Children of Long Ago* (poetry). Philomel, 1988

Audio Visual

Beall, Pamela Conn and Susan Hagen Nipp. *Wee Sing America.* Price Stern Sloan, 1987

Dana, Al. *All Time Favorite Dances.* Kimbo Educational, 1991 *(cassette)*

Discovering Washington, Our Nation's Capital (30 minutes) Film Ideas, 1988

Answer Key

Page 21

1. Martha Custis
2. two
3. Mount Vernon
4. army
5. Valley Forge
6. president
7. tax
8. farmer

Page 30

1. England or the British
2. to rescue a friend (Dr. Beanes)
3. a ship in the harbor
4. "The Defense of Fort McHenry"
5. "The Star-Spangled Banner"
6. 1931

Page 31

1. outside
2. flag
3. ground
4. flag
5. school
6. mourning
7. burning
8. colony

Answer: Old Glory

Page 41

Pages 42–43

1. White House
2. Capitol
3. Washington Monument
4. Jefferson Memorial
5. Lincoln Memorial
6. Statue of Liberty
7. Iwo Jima

Page 47

1. 6
2. 3
3. 8
4. 1
5. 4
6. 11
7. 8
8. 7
9. 8
10. 9
11. 4
12. 11
13. 12
seven red stripes, six white stripes

Page 48

twos–8, 14, 20, 24, 32, 38, 40, 46, 50
fives–15, 25, 30, 50
tens–20, 40

1. 16
2. 23
3. 32
4. 37
5. 8
6. 11
7. 25
8. 33
9. 9

Page 53

1. White House
2. Capitol
3. Washington Memorial
4. Jefferson Memorial
5. Lincoln Memorial
6. Statue of Liberty
7. Iwo Jima Memorial

Page 55

1. Connecticut
2. Delaware
3. Georgia
4. Maryland
5. Massachusetts
6. New Hampshire
7. New Jersey
8. New York
9. North Carolina
10. Pennsylvania
11. Rhode Island
12. South Carolina
13. Virginia

Page 56

1. District of Columbia
2. George Washington
3. John Adams
4. Thomas Jefferson
5. Capitol
6. White House

Page 73

1. T
2. F
3. T
4. F
5. F
6. T
7. T
8. T
9. T
10. T
11. F
12. T
13. F
14. T
15. T
16. F
17. T
18. T